THE LARK NOW LEAVES
HIS WAT'RY NEST

(SATB)

SIR WILLIAM DAVENANT

C. M. SHEARER

SC-87

B-372

Song Index on page 92

2

morn will nev-er rise Till she can dress your beau - ty at

morn will nev-er rise Till she can dress your beau - ty at

the morn will nev-er rise and dress your beau - ty at

the morn will nev-er rise and dress your beau - ty at

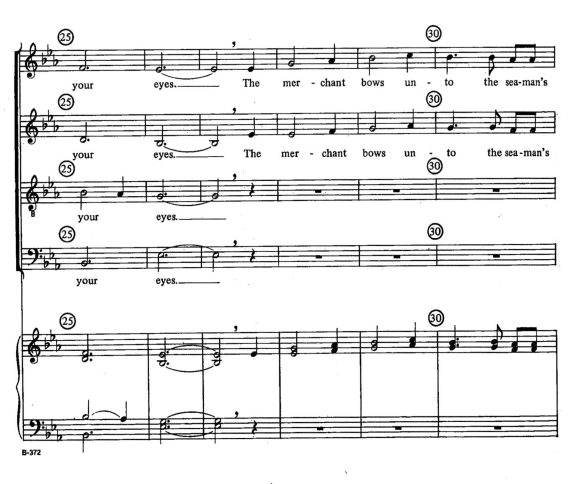

your eyes._____ The mer - chant bows un - to the sea-man's

your eyes._____ The mer - chant bows un - to the sea-man's

your eyes._____

your eyes._____

4

THE SPLENDOR FALLS

SATB
U.I.L. Sight Reading Selection for Class CCC (SATB)

TENNYSON

JACK BOYD

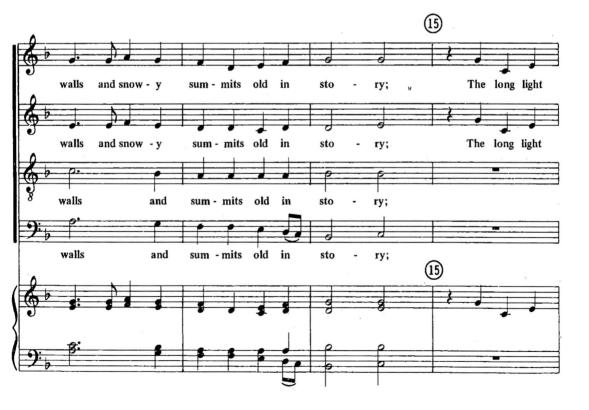

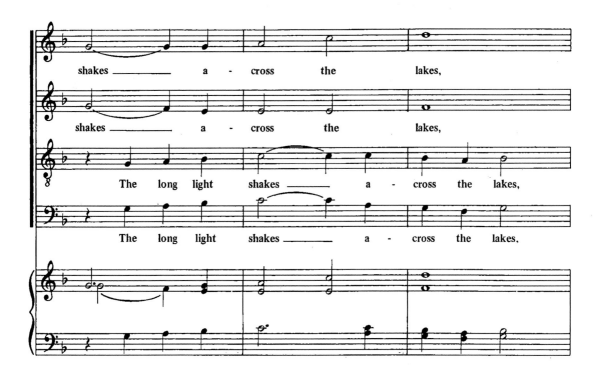

leaps in glo - ry, leaps — in — glo - ry.

leaps in glo - ry, leaps — in — glo - ry.

leaps in glo - ry, leaps in glo - ry.

leaps in glo - ry, leaps in glo - ry.

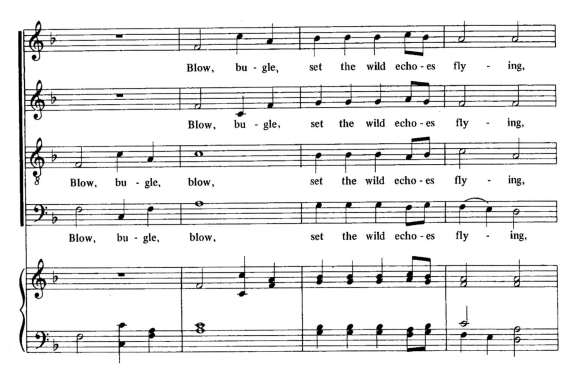

Blow, bu - gle, set the wild echo - es fly - ing,

Blow, bu - gle, set the wild echo - es fly - ing,

Blow, bu - gle, blow, set the wild echo - es fly - ing,

Blow, bu - gle, blow, set the wild echo - es fly - ing,

blow, bu - gle, blow; an - swer, echo - es, dy - ing,

blow, bu - gle, blow; an - swer, echo - es, dy - ing,

blow, bu - gle; an - swer, echo - es, dy - ing, now

blow, bu - gle; an - swer, echo - es, — dy - ing, now

dy - ing, dy - ing, dy - ing.

dy - ing, dy - ing, dy - ing.

dy - ing, now dy - ing, now dy - ing. ____

dy - ing, now dy - ing, now dy - ing. ____

TAKE, O TAKE THOSE LIPS AWAY
(SATB)

W. SHAKESPEARE*

C.M. SHEARER

* Possibly by John Fletcher

B-372

break of day, Lights that do mis - lead the morn.

break of day, Lights that do mis - lead the morn.

break of day, Lights that do mis - lead the morn.

break of day, Lights that do mis - lead the morn.

But my kiss - es bring a - gain seals of love,

But my kiss - es bring a - gain seals of love,

But my kiss - es bring a - gain seals of love,

But my kiss - es bring a - gain seals of love,

seals of love, though sealed in vain, sealed in vain.

seals of love though sealed in vain, sealed 'in vain.

seals of love though sealed in vain, sealed in vain.

seals of love though sealed in vain, sealed in vain.

Take, O take those lips a - way, those lips____ a - way.____

Take, O take those lips a - way, those lips____ a - way.

Take, O take those lips a - way, those lips____ a - way.____

Take, O take those lips a - way, those lips a - way.____

THE RAINY DAY

SATB
U.I.L. Sight Reading Selection for Classes A & AA (SATB)

HENRY W. LONGFELLOW (1807-1882)   C. M. SHEARER

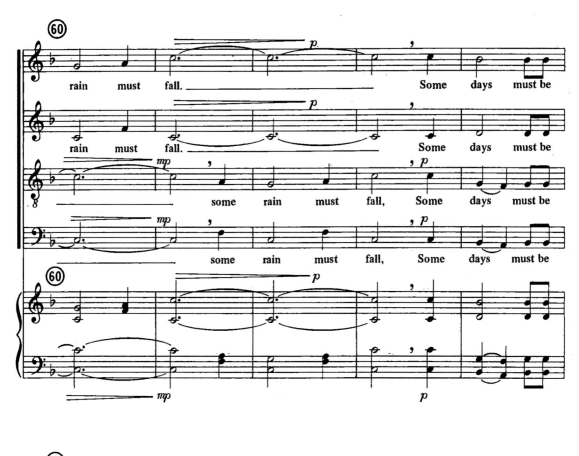

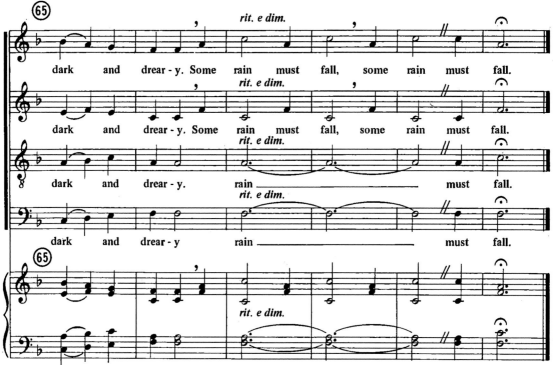

RIDING SONG

(U.I.L. Sight Reading Selection for Class A - AA and for
Class AAAA - AAAAA Second Group)

Anonymous

C.M. Shearer

B-372

Swing of waist and hip, Trot-ting down the twist-ed road With the world let
Com-rade, you and I, Care-less of the wea - ther Let-ting care go

Let us laugh to - geth - er, Mer - ry as of old,
slip.
by.

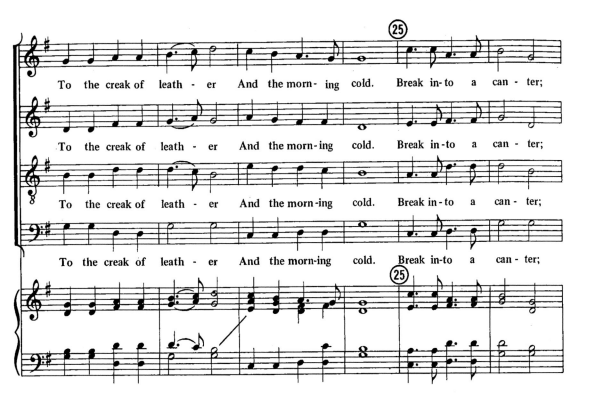

To the creak of leath - er And the morn- ing cold. Break in-to a can - ter;

To the creak of leath - er And the morn-ing cold. Break in-to a can - ter;

To the creak of leath - er And the morn-ing cold. Break in-to a can - ter;

To the creak of leath - er And the morn-ing cold. Break in-to a can - ter;

D. C. al Fine

Shout to bank and tree; Rock-ing down the wak - ing trail Stea - dy hand and knee.

Shout to bank and tree; Rock-ing down the wak - ing trail Stea - dy hand and knee.

Shout to bank and tree; Rock-ing down the wak - ing trail Stea - dy hand and knee.

Shout to bank and tree; Rock-ing down the wak - ing trail Stea - dy hand and knee.

D. C. al Fine

POOR MARINERS

U.I.L. Sight Reading Selection for Class A and AA (SATB)

THOMAS RAVENSCROFT

C. M. SHEARER

spend our lives in jeop - ar-dy,_ while o - thers live at ease:_____
we care for those mer-chant men, which do our states main - tain._____
he that is a bul - ly boy, come pledge me on the ground._____

spend our lives in jeop - ar-dy, while o - thers live at ease:_____
we care for those mer-chant men, which do our states main - tain._____
he that is a bul - ly boy, come pledge me on the ground.__

spend our lives in jeop - ar-dy, while o - thers live at ease:
we care for those mer-chant men, which do our states main - tain.
he that is a bul - ly boy, come pledge me on the ground.

spend our lives in jeop - ar-dy, while o - thers live at ease:
we care for those mer-chant men, which do our states main - tain.
he that is a bul - ly boy, come pledge me on the ground.

Chorus ⑩

Shall we go dance the round, the round, the round, and shall we go dance the

Shall we go dance the round, the round, the round, and shall we go dance_the

Shall we go dance the round, the round, the round, and shall we go dance the

Shall we go dance the round, the round, the round, and shall we go dance the

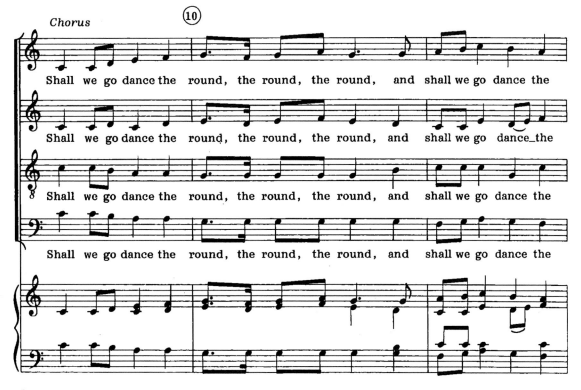

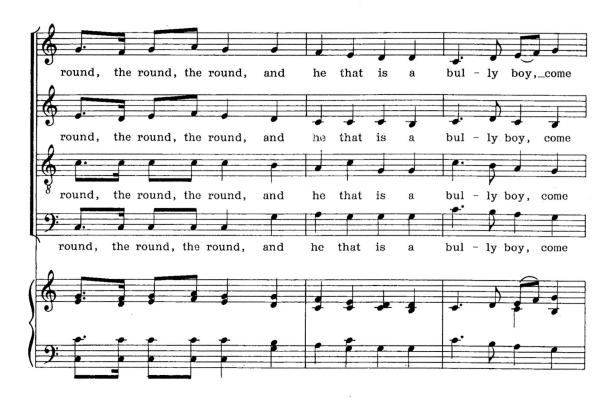

round, the round, the round, and he that is a bul - ly boy,—come

round, the round, the round, and he that is a bul - ly boy, come

round, the round, the round, and he that is a bul - ly boy, come

round, the round, the round, and he that is a bul - ly boy, come

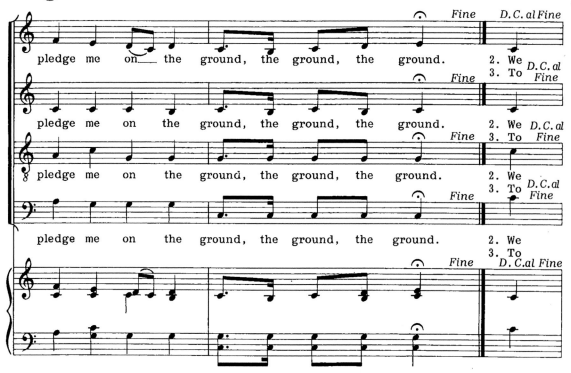

⑮

pledge me on— the ground, the ground, the ground. 2. We
3. To

pledge me on the ground, the ground, the ground. 2. We
3. To

pledge me on the ground, the ground, the ground. 2. We
3. To

pledge me on the ground, the ground, the ground. 2. We
3. To

Fine   D.C. al Fine

NEW PRINCE, NEW POMP

SATB

U.I.L. Sight Reading Selection for Class AAA (SATB).

ROBERT SOUTHWELL (1561-1595)

C. M. SHEARER

B-372

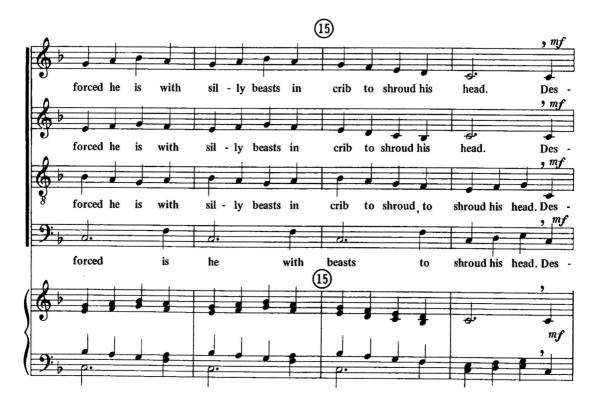

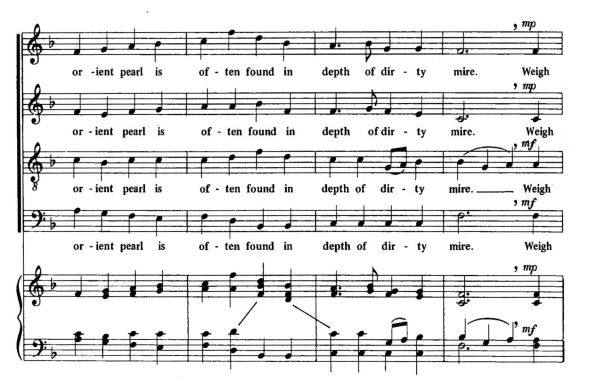

pise him not for ly - ing there, first, what he is in - quire; An

pise him not for ly - ing there, first, what he is in - quire; _____ An

pise him not for ly - ing there, first, what he is in - quire; _____ An

pise him not for ly - ing there, first, what he is in - quire; An _____

or - ient pearl is of - ten found in depth of dir - ty mire. Weigh

or - ient pearl is of - ten found in depth of dir - ty mire. Weigh

or - ient pearl is of - ten found in depth of dir - ty mire. _____ Weigh

or - ient pearl is of - ten found in depth of dir - ty mire. Weigh

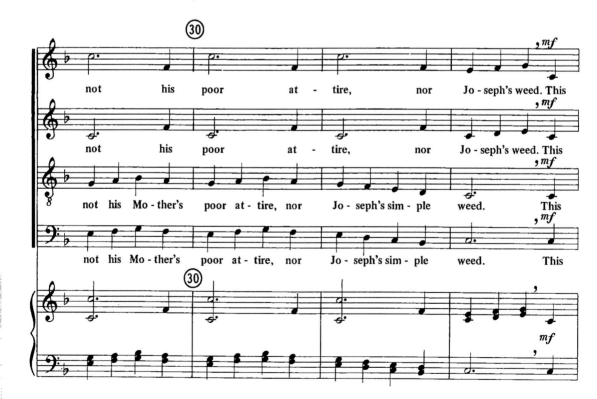

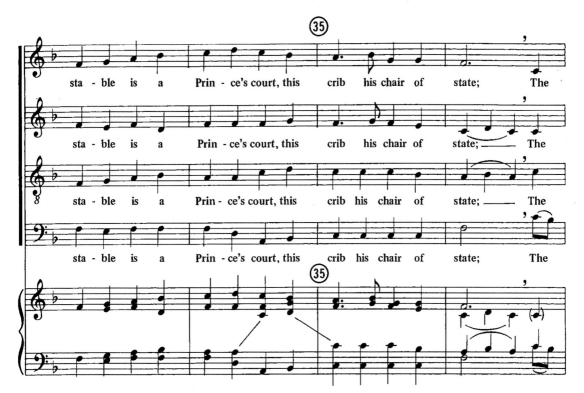

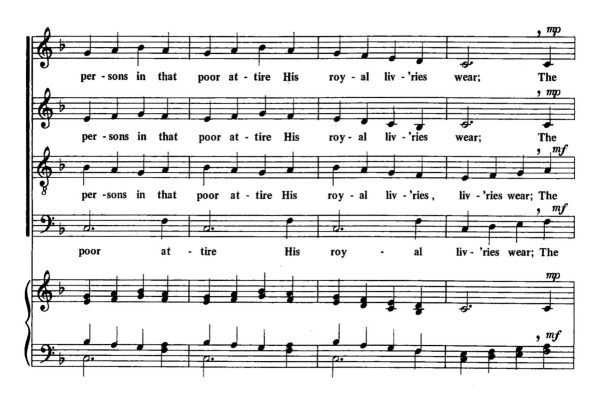

Hark! the Vesper Hymn Is Stealing

U.I.L. Sight Reading Selection for Class AAA

THOMAS MOORE   **C. M. SHEARER**

Hark! the ves - per hymn is__ steal - ing O'er the wa - ters__

34

B-372

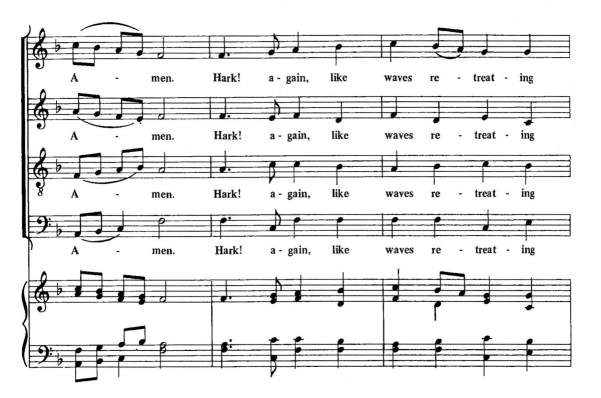

A - men. Hark! a - gain, like waves re - treat - ing

A - men. Hark! a - gain, like waves re - treat - ing

A - men. Hark! a - gain, like waves re - treat - ing

A - men. Hark! a - gain, like waves re - treat - ing

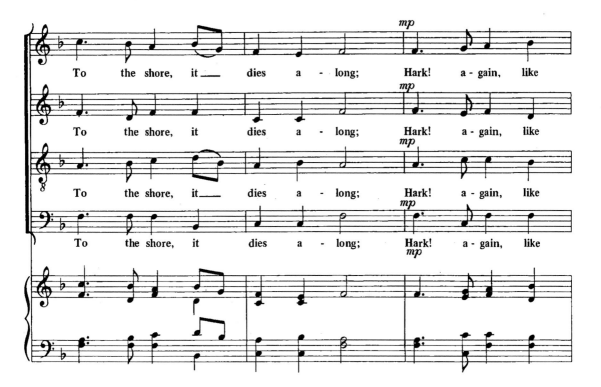

To the shore, it___ dies a - long; Hark! a - gain, like

To the shore, it dies a - long; Hark! a - gain, like

To the shore, it___ dies a - long; Hark! a - gain, like

To the shore, it dies a - long; Hark! a - gain, like

waves re - treat - ing, To the shore, it ___ dies a - long.

waves re - treat - ing, To the shore, it dies a - long.

waves re - treat - ing, To the shore, it ___ dies a - long.

waves re - treat - ing, To the shore, it dies a - long.

mf-f *Second time cresc. and ritard.*

Ju - bi - la - te, ju - bi - la - te, ju - bi - la - te, A - men.

Ju - bi - la - te, ju - bi - la - te, ju - bi - la - te, A - men.

Ju - bi - la - te,__ ju - bi - la - te,__ ju - bi - la - te,__ A - men.

Ju - bi - la - te,__ ju - bi - la - te,__ ju - bi - la - te,__ A - men.

GATHER YOUR ROSEBUDS

U.I.L. Sight Reading Selection for Class AAA (SATB)

ROBERT HERRICK   **C. M. SHEARER**

1. Ga - ther your rose-buds while you___ may, Old time is still a -
2. The glo-rious lamp of heaven, the___ sun, The high - er he's_ a -
3. That age is best that is the___ first, While youth and blood are___

PACK, CLOUDS, AWAY
(for SATB Choir)

THOMAS HEYWOOD

C. M. SHEARER

25

row; Bird, prune thy wing; and night - in - gale, sing, To give my

mf

row; Bird, prune thy wing; and night - in - gale, sing, To give my

mf

row; Bird, prune thy wing; and night - in - gale, sing, To give my

mf

row; Bird, prune thy wing; and night - in - gale, sing, To give my

mf

30

f

love ___ good mor - row, To give my love good mor -

f

love ___ good mor - row, To give my love good mor -

f

love ___ good ___ mor - row, To give my love good mor

f

love ___ good ___ mor - row, To give my love good mor

f

THE WATER BEETLE

SATB.
U.I.L. Sight Reading Selection, Classes
AAA - Mixed (SATB), AA-A - Mixed (SATB) AA-A Mixed (SAB).

HILAIRE BELLOC

C.M. SHEARER

B-372

*The canon (measures 16 thru 22) may be omitted.

THE SPLENDOUR FALLS

(SATB)

(U.I.L. Sight Reading Selection for Class AAA)

Tennyson

C.M. Shearer

Verse 2 O, hark! O, hear! how thin and clear,
And thinner, clearer, farther, going!
O, sweet and far from cliff and scar
The horns of Elfland are blowing!
Blow, bugle, blow, now let us hear
The purple glens sweet sound replying:
Blow, bugle, blow, (etc. as in Vs. 1)

Verse 3 O, love they die in yon rich sky
They faint on hill or field or river:
Our echoes roll from soul to soul
And grow for ever and ever.
Blow, bugle, blow (etc. as in Vs 1)

long light shakes a-cross the lake, And the wild cat-a-ract leaps in glo - ry. Blow,

long light shakes a-cross the lake, And the wild cat-a-ract leaps in glo - ry. Blow,

long light shakes a-cross the lake, And the wild cat-a-ract leaps in glo - ry. Blow,

long light shakes a-cross the lake, And the wild cat-a-ract leaps in glo - ry. Blow,

(5)

bu-gle, blow, blow, bu-gle, blow, set the wild, wild ech - oes fly - ing, fly - ing, Blow,

bu-gle, blow, blow, bu-gle, blow, set the wild, wild ech - oes fly - ing, fly - ing, Blow,

bu-gle, blow, blow, bu-gle, blow, set the wild, wild ech - oes fly - ing, fly - - - - - - - - - - - -

bu-gle, blow, blow, bu-gle, blow, set the wild, wild ech - oes fly - ing, fly - - - - - - - - - - - -

(5)

B-372

54

How Lovely is Thy Dwelling Place

SCOTTISH PSALTER, 1650

SATB

EMILY CROCKER

U.I.L Sight Reading Selection for Class AAA & CCC (Mixed)

B-372

To the Glory of the Father

U.I.L. Sight Reading Selection for Class AAAA and Class AAAAA Second Groups

GERARD MANLEY HOPKINS

C. M. SHEARER

In the shar-ing of thy__ mys-ter-ies; And ev-ery
In the shar-ing of thy mys-ter-ies; And ev-ery
shows, In the shar-ing of thy__ mys-ter-ies;
shows, And ev-ery

pow-er__ in us is A-gainst__ thy pow-er put un-der
pow-er in us is A-gainst__ thy pow-er put un-der
A-gainst__ thy pow-er put un-der
pow-er__ in us is A-gainst__ thy pow-er put un-der

feet In the Ho - ly Ghost the Par - a - clete To the glo -
feet In the Ho - ly Ghost the Par - a - clete To the glo -
feet In the Ho - ly Ghost the Par - a - clete
feet In the Ho - ly Ghost the Par - a - clete

ry,___ the glo - ry, the glo - ry of the Fa -
ry,___ the glo - ry,___ the glo - ry of the Fa -
To the glo - ry,___ the glo - ry of the Fa -
To the glo - ry,___ the glo - ry of the Fa -

THOSE EVENING BELLS

SATB

U.I.L. Sight Reading Selection for Class AAAA (SATB)

THOMAS MOORE (1779-1852)   **C. M. SHEARER**

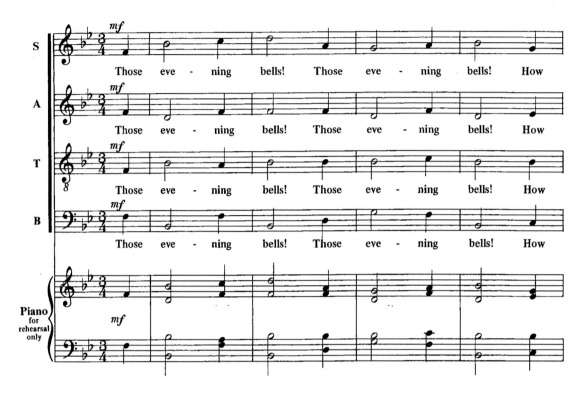

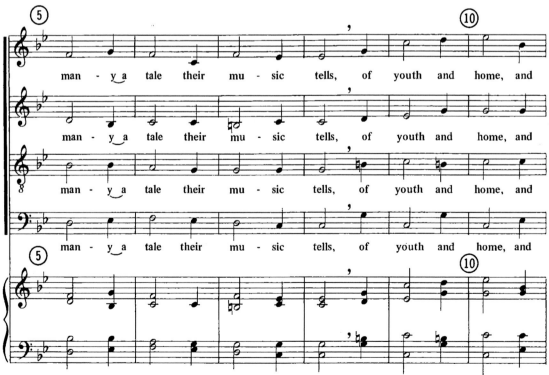

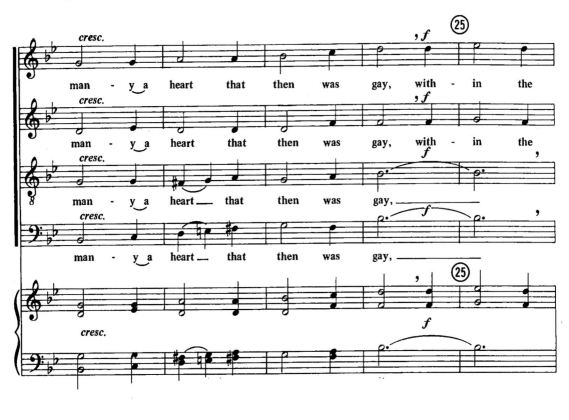

eve - ning bells. And so 'twill be when I am gone, that

eve - ning bells. And so 'twill be when I am gone, that

eve - ning bells.

eve - ning bells.

tune - ful peal will still ring on,

tune - ful peal will still ring on,

While oth - er bards shall

While oth - er bards shall

Ah, Fading Shadow

U.I.L. Sight Reading Selection for Class AAAA

DEANA COLLINS

C. M. SHEARER

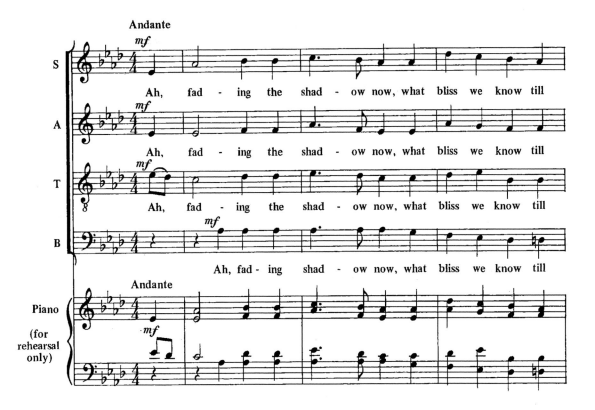

B-372

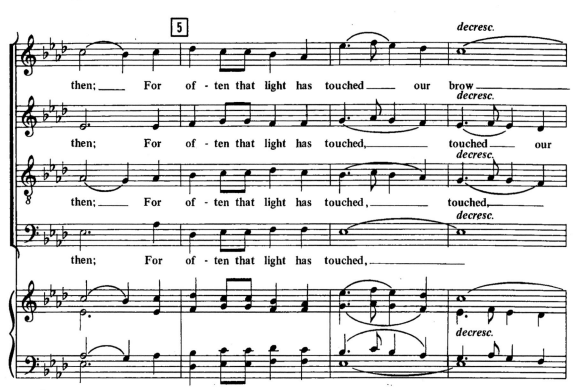

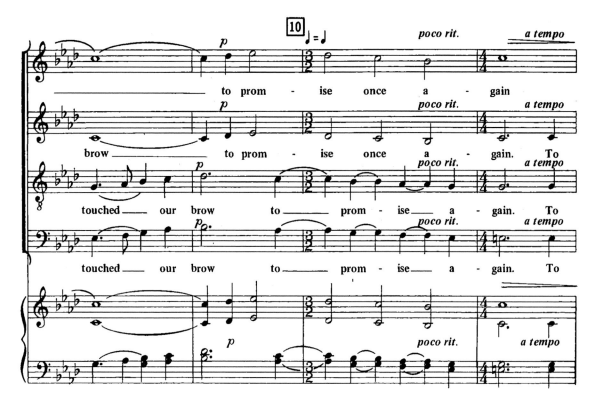

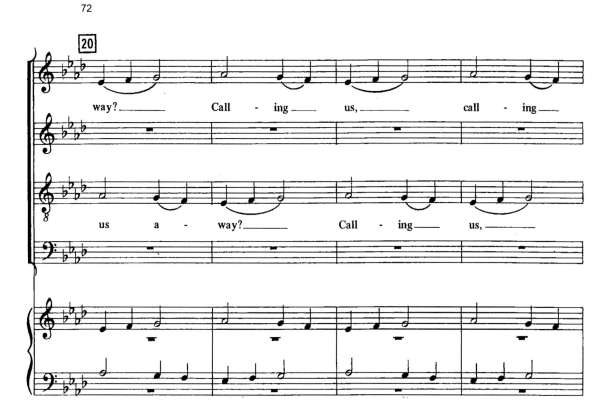

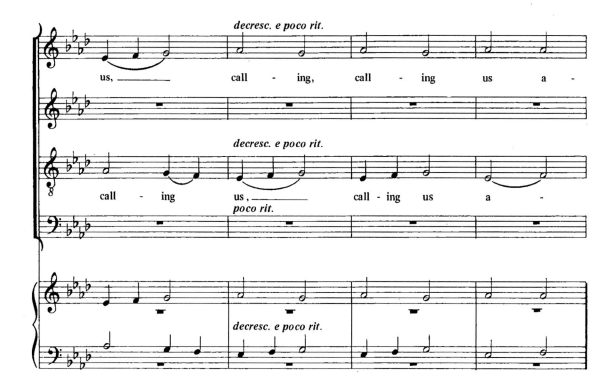

I HAVE BEEN HERE BEFORE

U.I.L. Sight Reading Selection for Class AAAA Mixed (SATB).

D. G. ROSSETTI

C. M. SHEARER

THE HARP THAT ONCE THROUGH TARA'S HALLS

SATB

U.I.L. Sight Reading Selection for Class AAAAA (SATB)

THOMAS MOORE (1779-1852)   C. M. SHEARER

Wind Through the Olive Trees

SATB

U.I.L. Sight Reading Selection for Class AAAAA

UNKNOWN

C. M. SHEARER

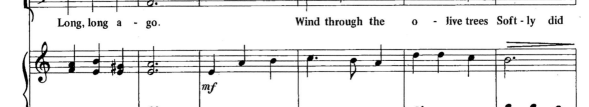

The bass part may be omitted from bars 26 - 33.

* *Crescendo only if optional cut is observed.*

Song Index

1. LARK NOW LEAVES HIS WAT'RY NEST, THE, Shearer 1
2. SPLENDOR FALLS, THE, Boyd 6
3. TAKE, O TAKE THOSE LIPS AWAY, Shearer 11
4. RAINY DAY, THE, Shearer 14
5. RIDING SONG, Shearer 19
6. POOR MARINERS, Shearer 22
7. NEW PRINCE, NEW POMP, Shearer 25
8. HARK! THE VESPER HYMN IS STEALING, Shearer 32
9. GATHER YE ROSEBUDS, Shearer 39
10. PACK, CLOUDS, AWAY, Shearer 42
11. WATER BEETLE, THE, Shearer 49
12. SPLENDOUR FALLS, THE, Shearer 52
13. HOW LOVELY IS THY DWELLING PLACE, Crocker 55
14. TO THE GLORY OF THE FATHER, Shearer 58
15. THOSE EVENING BELLS, Shearer 64
16. AH, FADING SHADOW, Shearer 69
17. I HAVE BEEN HERE BEFORE, Shearer 74
18. HARP THAT ONCE THROUGH TARA'S HALLS, THE, Shearer 81
19. WIND THROUGH THE OLIVE TREES, Shearer ... 86